This book was written for men, although it can certainly benefit the entire family.

Quite simply it is a "daily reading" book designed to get your day started in the right direction.

Each day has a passage from one of the Psalms coupled with a thought for the day. The underlined word and associated picture are intended to give you a word to meditate on for that day.

My prayer for you is that Psalms of Celebration would be a simple reminder to CELEBRATE each and every day.

Duderonomy can be used for:
A morning devotional thought
A late night meditation
A family dinner devotional thought

It's a great day to Celebrate!
Jay Laffoon

I would like to thank the following people for their assistance with this book:
- Jeff Huisjen for thinking of Duderonomy. What a great title.
- Shana Laffoon for her fantastic creative eye in picking out the images.
- Diane Laffoon for her superior layout and graphic talents.
- My wife Laura and entire family who give me reason to rejoice everyday!

# Psalm 1

*"Blessed is the man whose delight is in the law of the LORD, and on his law he meditates day and night. He is like a tree planted by streams of water, which yields its fruit in season and whose leaf does not wither. Whatever he does prospers."*

Commit your way to the Lord today and he will direct your path!

# Psalm 2

*"Serve the LORD with fear and rejoice with trembling... Blessed are all who take refuge in Him."*

Let Christ be your refuge
from the storms of life!

# Psalm 3

*"May your blessing be on your people."*

Receive the blessing of God's Grace today!

# Psalm 4

*"Know that the Lord has set apart the godly for Himself, the LORD will hear when I call to Him."*

Set yourself apart for the Lord.

# Psalm 5

*"In the morning, O LORD, you hear my voice; in the morning I lay my requests before you and wait in expectation."*

He is waiting to answer your requests!

# Psalm 6

*"Be merciful to me, LORD, for I am faint; O LORD, heal me, for my bones are in agony."*

The Lord gives strength to the faint, seek His strength!

# Psalm 7

*"O righteous God, who searches minds and hearts, bring to an end the violence of the wicked and make the righteous secure."*

Rest in the secure arms of our righteous God.

# Psalm 8

*"O LORD, our Lord, how majestic is your name in all the earth! You have set your glory above the heavens."*

Proclaim His majesty!

# Psalm 9

*"I will be glad and rejoice in you; I will sing praise to your name, O Most High."*

Choose gladness today because of what Christ has done!

# Psalm 10

*"Arise, LORD! Lift up your hand, O God. Do not forget the helpless."*

Pray for the Lord's hand in the lives of the helpless in your life.

# Psalm 11

*"The LORD is in His holy temple; the LORD is on His heavenly throne. He observes the sons of men; His eyes examine them. The LORD examines the righteous."*

Rejoice His eye is on YOU today!

# Psalm 12

*"And the words of the LORD are flawless, like silver refined in a furnace of clay, purified seven times."*

Listen for the words of the Lord in your life!

# Psalm 13

*"But I trust in Your unfailing love; my heart rejoices in Your salvation. I will sing to the LORD, for He has been good to me."*

Sing to the Lord for the goodness in your life.

# Psalm 14

*"The LORD looks down from heaven on the sons of men to see if there are any who understand, any who seek God."*

Seek the Lord and He will be found by you!

# Psalm 15

*"LORD who may dwell in Your sanctuary? Who may live on Your holy hill? He whose walk is blameless and who does what is righteous, who speaks the truth..."*

Walk blamelessly before the Lord and dwell in His presence.

# Psalm 16

*"I have set the LORD always before me. Because He is at my right hand, I will not be shaken. Therefore my heart is glad and my tongue rejoices; my body also will rest secure."*

Rest secure in the Lord.

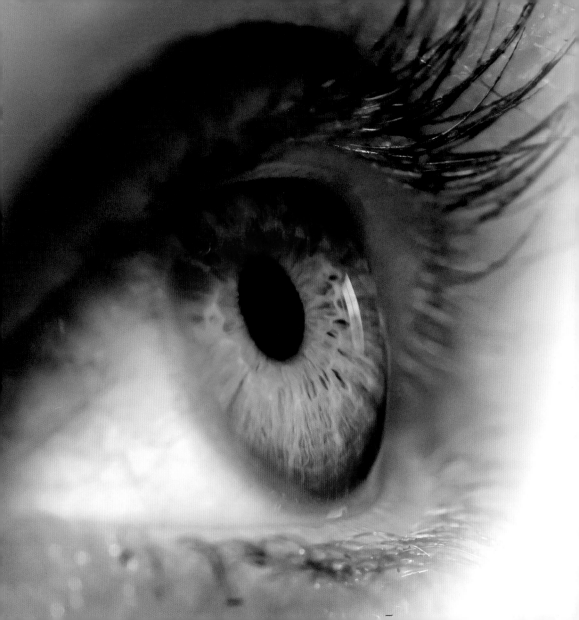

# Psalm 17

*"Keep me as the apple of Your eye."*

YOU are the apple of His eye!

# Psalm 18

*"I love you, O LORD, my strength. The LORD is my rock, my fortress and my deliverer; my God is my rock, in whom I take refuge. He is my shield and the horn of my salvation, my stronghold."*

Today tell the Lord... "I Love You!"

# Psalm 19

*"The heavens declare the glory of God; the skies proclaim the work of His hands."*

Look to the heavens - declare to the Lord how majestic are His works.

# Psalm 20

*"May the LORD answer you when you are in distress; may the name of the God of Jacob protect you."*

What is distressing you today? Seek the protection of the God of Jacob.

# Psalm 21

*"For the king trusts in the LORD; through the unfailing love of the Most High he will not be shaken."*

May your day be unshakable as you trust in the Lord.

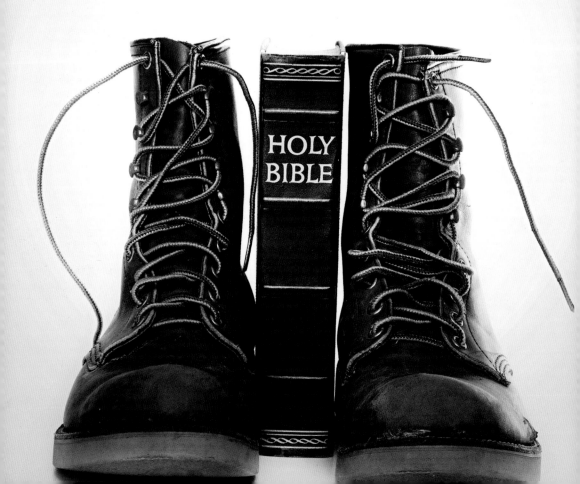

# Psalm 22

*"I will declare Your name to my brothers; in the congregation I will praise You. You who fear the LORD, praise Him! All you descendants of Jacob, honor Him! Revere Him, all you descendants of Israel!"*

Revere, Honor and Praise the Lord today!

# Psalm 23

*"The LORD is my shepherd, I shall not be in want. He makes me lie down in green pastures, He leads me beside quiet waters, He restores my soul. He guides me in paths of righteousness for His name's sake. Even though I walk through the valley of the shadow of death, I will fear no evil, for You are with me; Your rod and Your staff, they comfort me. You prepare a table before me in the presence of my enemies. You anoint my head with oil; my cup overflows."*

Surely goodness and love will follow me all the days of my life, and I will dwell in the house of the LORD forever.

# Psalm 24

*"Who is this King of glory? The LORD strong and mighty, the LORD mighty in battle. Lift up your heads, O you gates; lift them up, you ancient doors, that the King of glory may come in. Who is He, this King of glory? The LORD Almighty - He is the King of glory."*

Rejoice! The LORD Almighty is the King of glory.

# Psalm 25

*"Show me Your ways, O LORD, teach me Your paths; guide me in Your truth and teach me, for You are God my Savior, and my hope is in You all day long."*

Walk today in the paths of the Lord.

You shall know the Truth and the Truth will make you free!

# Psalm 27

*"The LORD is my light and my salvation - whom shall I fear? The LORD is the stronghold of my life - of whom shall I be afraid?"*

Perfect Love casts out all fear.
The Lord loves you perfectly!

# Psalm 28

*"The LORD is my strength and my shield; my heart trusts in Him, and I am helped. My heart leaps for joy and I will give thanks to Him in song. The LORD is the strength of His people, a fortress of salvation for His anointed one. Save Your people and bless Your inheritance; be their shepherd and carry them forever."*

Jesus the Good Shepherd will carry you.

# Psalm 29

*"The voice of the LORD strikes with flashes of lightning. The voice of the LORD shakes the desert; the LORD shakes the Desert of Kadesh. The voice of the LORD twists the oaks and strips the forests bare."*

Listen for the voice of the Lord today.

# Psalm 30

*"Sing to the LORD, you saints of His; praise His holy name."*

Sing a song of praise to the Lord as you walk through this day.

# Psalm 31

*"Let Your face shine on Your servant; save me in Your unfailing love."*

Bask in His unfailing love.

# Psalm 32

*"Rejoice in the LORD and be glad, you righteous; sing, all you who are upright in heart!"*

May your heart be upright this and every day.

# Psalm 33

*"For the word of the LORD is right and true; He is faithful in all He does."*

He is faithful to you!

# Psalm 34

*"Glorify the LORD with me; let us exalt His name together."*

Exalt Him today.

# Psalm 35

*"My whole being will exclaim, "Who is like You, O LORD? You rescue the poor from those too strong for them, the poor and needy from those who rob them."*

May He rescue you in your time of need.

# Psalm 36

*"Your love, O LORD, reaches to the heavens, Your faithfulness to the skies. Your righteousness is like the mighty mountains, Your justice like the great deep."*

Awesome is our Lord.

# Psalm 37

*"Trust in the LORD and do good; dwell in the land and enjoy safe pasture. Delight yourself in the LORD and He will give you the desires of your heart. Commit your way to the LORD; trust in Him."*

He longs to make your heart His.

# Psalm 38

*"O LORD, do not forsake me; be not far from me, O my God. Come quickly to help me, O Lord my Savior."*

He is close to you.

# Psalm 39

*"My hope is in You. Save me from all my transgressions; do not make me the scorn of fools."*

Place your hope in Him.

# Psalm 40

*"I waited patiently for the LORD; He turned to me and heard my cry. He lifted me out of the slimy pit, out of the mud and mire; He set my feet on a rock and gave me a firm place to stand. He put a new song in my mouth, a hymn of praise to our God. Many will see and fear and put their trust in the LORD."*

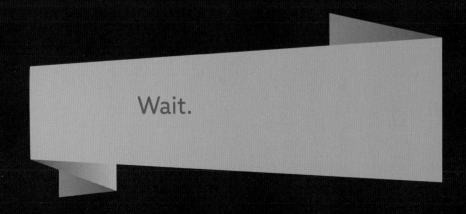

Wait.

# Psalm 41

*"Praise be to the LORD, the God of Israel, from everlasting to everlasting. Amen and Amen."*

Praise the everlasting Lord.

# Psalm 42

*"As the deer pants for streams of water, so my soul pants for you, O God. My soul thirsts for God, for the living God. When can I go and meet with God?"*

Meet Him in your heart today.

# Psalm 43

*"Send forth Your light and Your truth, let them guide me; let them bring me to Your holy mountain, to the place where You dwell."*

Walk in the light as He is in the light.

# Psalm 44

*"In God we make our boast all day long, and we will praise your name forever. Selah"*

May your confidence be in the Lord.

# Psalm 45

*"Your throne, O God, will last for ever and ever; a scepter of justice will be the scepter of Your kingdom."*

May you worship at the throne of God today.

# Psalm 46

*"God is our refuge and strength, an ever-present help in trouble. Therefore we will not fear, though the earth give way and the mountains fall into the heart of the sea, though its waters roar and foam and the mountains quake with their surging."*

Rest in the strength of the Lord.

"Clap your hands, all you nations; shout to God with cries of joy. How awesome is the LORD Most High, the great King over all the earth!"

Like a child, clap and sing to the Lord.

*"This God is our God for ever and ever; He will be our guide even to the end."*

Trust in His sure, guiding hand.

# Psalm 49

*"But God will redeem my life from the grave; He will surely take me to Himself. Selah"*

Our redeemer lives!

# Psalm 50

*"He who sacrifices thank offerings honors me, and He prepares the way so that I may show Him the salvation of God."*

May your heart overflow with thankfulness to the Lord.

# Psalm 51

*"Create in me a pure heart, O God, and renew a steadfast spirit within me. Do not cast me from Your presence or take Your Holy Spirit from me. Restore to me the joy of Your salvation and grant me a willing spirit, to sustain me."*

The Lord will restore your joy!

# Psalm 52

*"But I am like an olive tree flourishing in the house of God; I trust in God's unfailing love for ever and ever."*

Trust in the Lord.

# Psalm 53

*"God looks down from heaven on the sons of men to see if there are any who understand, any who seek God."*

Seek the Lord with your whole heart.

# Psalm 54

*"Surely God is my help; the Lord is the one who sustains me."*

He will sustain you!

# Psalm 55

*"But I call to God, and the LORD saves me. Evening, morning and noon I cry out in distress, and He hears my voice. He ransoms me unharmed from the battle waged against me, even though many oppose me."*

Call upon the Lord.

# Psalm 56

*"In God, whose word I praise, in the LORD, whose word I praise - in God I trust; I will not be afraid. What can man do to me?"*

Trust in God and fear not.

"Have mercy on me, O God, have mercy on me, for in You my soul takes refuge. I will take refuge in the shadow of Your wings until the disaster has passed. I cry out to God Most High, to God, who fulfills for me."

May mercy be by your side.

# Psalm 58

*"Then men will say, 'Surely the righteous still are rewarded; surely there is a God who judges the earth.'"*

Walk in righteousness.

# Psalm 59

*"But I will sing of Your strength, in the morning I will sing of Your love; for You are my fortress, my refuge in times of trouble. O my Strength, I sing praise to You; You, O God, are my fortress, my loving God."*

Sing to the Lord a new song, celebrate!

# Psalm 60

*"Save us and help us with Your right hand, that those You love may be delivered."*

He is your hope and deliverer.

"I long to dwell in Your tent forever and take refuge in the shelter of Your wings. Selah"

May heaven be your home.

"Find rest, O my soul, in God alone; my hope comes from Him. He alone is my rock and my salvation; He is my fortress, I will not be shaken. My salvation and my honor depend on God; He is my mighty rock, my refuge. Trust in Him at all times, O people; pour out your hearts to Him, for God is our refuge."

Pour out your heart to the Lord.

# Psalm 63

*"Because Your love is better than life, my lips will glorify You. I will praise You as long as I live, and in Your name I will lift up my hands."*

Let your lips glorify the Lord.

# Psalm 64

*"Let the righteous rejoice in the LORD and take refuge in Him; let all the upright in heart praise Him!"*

In your heart be upright and rejoice!

# Psalm 65

*"Blessed are those You choose and bring near to live in Your courts! We are filled with the good things of Your house, of Your holy temple."*

Be filled with the goodness of the Lord.

# Psalm 66

*"Shout with joy to God, all the earth! Sing the glory of His name; make His praise glorious!"*

Glorify the Lord!

# Psalm 67

*"May God be gracious to us and bless us and make His face shine upon us. Selah"*

Receive the blessing of the Lord today.

# Psalm 68

*"Praise be to the Lord, to God our Savior,*
*who daily bears our burdens."*

Cast all your burdens on Him.

# Psalm 69

*"Answer me, O LORD, out of the goodness of Your love; in Your great mercy turn to me."*

His love and mercy await.

# Psalm 70

*"But may all who seek You rejoice and be glad in You; may those who love Your salvation always say, 'Let God be exalted!'"*

Exalt His holy name!

# Psalm 71

*"My mouth is filled with Your praise, declaring Your splendor all day long."*

Declare the splendor of the Lord.

# Psalm 72

*"Praise be to the LORD God, the God of Israel, who alone does marvelous deeds. Praise be to His glorious name forever, may the whole earth be filled with His glory. Amen and Amen."*

Praise Him, Praise Him, Praise Him!

# Psalm 73

*"But as for me, it is good to be near God."*

Draw near to the Lord.

# Psalm 74

*"But You, O God, are my king from of old; You bring salvation upon the earth."*

Salvation is from the Lord!

# Psalm 75

*"As for me, I will declare this forever; I will sing praise to the God of Jacob."*

Sing a song of praise to the Lord.

# Psalm 76

*"You are resplendent with light, more majestic than mountains."*

Majesty, worship His majesty.

# Psalm 77

*"I will remember the deeds of the LORD; yes, I will remember Your miracles of long ago. I will meditate on all Your works and consider all Your mighty deeds. Your ways, O God, are holy."*

Consider the blessings the Lord has granted you.

# Psalm 78

*"He built His sanctuary like the heights, like the earth that He established forever."*

Seek the sanctuary of the Lord today.

# Psalm 79

"Then we Your people, the sheep of Your pasture, will praise You forever; from generation to generation we will recount Your praise."

Praise the name of Jesus.

# Psalm 80

*"Restore us, O LORD God Almighty; make Your face shine upon us, that we may be saved."*

Seek the Lord and be saved!

# Psalm 81

*"Sing for joy to God our strength; shout aloud to the God of Jacob! Begin the music, strike the tambourine, play the melodious harp and lyre."*

May your heart be filled with the music of the Lord.

# Psalm 82

*"Rise up, O God, judge the earth, for all the nations are Your inheritance."*

He reigns!

# Psalm 83

*"Let them know that You, whose name is the LORD
- that You alone are the Most High over all the earth."*

Praise the Most High God.

# Psalm 84

*"How lovely is Your dwelling place,*
*O LORD Almighty!"*

Dwell in the house of the Lord.

# Psalm 85

*"I will listen to what God the LORD will say;
He promises peace to His people, His saints."*

Rejoice in the promise of peace.

# Psalm 86

*"Guard my life, for I am devoted to You. You are my God; save Your servant who trusts in you."*

Trust in the Lord.

# Psalm 87

*"He has set His foundation on the holy mountain."*

May your foundation be on the rock.

# Psalm 88

*"O LORD, the God who saves me, day and night I cry out before You."*

He is salvation!

# Psalm 89

*"I will sing of the LORD's great love forever; with my mouth I will make Your faithfulness known through all generations."*

He is faithful.

# Psalm 90

*"Teach us to number our days aright, that we may gain a heart of wisdom."*

Seek the wisdom of the Lord.

# Psalm 91

*"I will say of the LORD, 'He is my refuge and my fortress, my God, in whom I trust.'"*

He's my rock, He's my fortress,
He's my deliverer in Him will I trust.

# Psalm 92

*"It is good to praise the LORD and make music to Your name, O Most High, to proclaim Your love in the morning and Your faithfulness at night."*

Proclaim love and faithfulness today.

# Psalm 93

*"Your statutes stand firm; holiness adorns Your house for endless days, O LORD."*

Walk in holiness.

# Psalm 94

*"For the LORD will not reject His people; He will never forsake His inheritance."*

You are the Lord's inheritance.

# Psalm 95

*"For the LORD is the great God, the great King above all gods."*

Worship His greatness!

# Psalm 96

*"Sing to the LORD a new song; sing to the LORD, all the earth. Sing to the LORD, praise His name; proclaim his salvation day after day."*

Sing! Sing! Sing!

# Psalm 97

*"For You, O LORD, are the Most High over all the earth; You are exalted far above all gods."*

Exalt His name forever.

# Psalm 98

*"Shout for joy to the LORD, all the earth,*
*burst into jubilant song with music!"*

May your life burst with joy today!

# Psalm 99

*"Exalt the LORD our God and worship at His footstool; He is holy."*

He is Abba Father, worship at His holy feet.

# Psalm 100

*"Enter His gates with thanksgiving and His courts with praise; give thanks to Him and praise His name."*

Give thanks with a grateful heart.

# Psalm 101

*"I will be careful to lead a blameless life -
when will You come to me? I will walk in
my house with a blameless heart."*

May your heart be blameless today.

# Psalm 102

*"But You, O LORD, sit enthroned forever; Your renown endures through all generations."*

Trust in the One who sits on the throne!

# Psalm 103

*"Praise the LORD, O my soul; all my inmost being, praise His holy name. Praise the LORD, O my soul, and forget not all His benefits."*

Praise the Lord for the benefits of His love.

# Psalm 104

*"Praise the LORD, O my soul. O LORD my God, You are very great; You are clothed with splendor and majesty."*

Meditate on the splendor of the Lord.

# Psalm 105

*"Give thanks to the LORD, call on His name; make known among the nations what He has done. Sing to Him, sing praise to Him; tell of all His wonderful acts."*

The Lord is waiting for your call.

# Psalm 106

*"Praise the LORD. Give thanks to the LORD, for He is good; His love endures forever."*

May the enduring love of the Lord overwhelm your heart and soul.

# Psalm 107

*"Let them give thanks to the LORD for His unfailing love and His wonderful deeds for men, for He satisfies the thirsty and fills the hungry with good things."*

Think of all the good things the Lord has given you.

# Psalm 108

*"My heart is steadfast, O God; I will sing and make music with all my soul. Awake, harp and lyre! I will awaken the dawn."*

Set your heart steadfast on the Lord.

# Psalm 109

*"With my mouth I will greatly extol the LORD: in the great throng I will praise Him."*

Praise the Lord with your mouth, speak it out loud.

# Psalm 110

*"The LORD says to my Lord: 'Sit at my right hand until I make your enemies a footstool for your feet.'"*

Be still and watch
what the Lord will do!

# Psalm 111

*"The works of His hands are faithful and just;
all His precepts are trustworthy."*

God works in mysterious ways.

# Psalm 112

*"Praise the LORD. Blessed is the man who fears the LORD, who finds great delight in His commands."*

Fear Him and be blessed.

# Psalm 113

*"From the rising of the sun to the place where it sets, the name of the LORD is to be praised."*

Praise Him all day long.

# Psalm 114

*"Tremble, O earth, at the presence of the Lord, at the presence of the God of Jacob."*

In fear and trembling walk in His presence.

# Psalm 115

*"O house of Israel, trust in the LORD - He is their help and shield. O house of Aaron, trust in the LORD - He is their help and shield. You who fear Him, trust in the Lord - He is their help and shield."*

He will shield and protect you this day.

# Psalm 116

*"The LORD is gracious and righteous;*
*our God is full of compassion."*

May the compassion of the Lord
be yours today.

# Psalm 117

*"Praise the LORD, all you nations; extol Him, all you peoples. For great is His love toward us, and the faithfulness of the LORD endures forever. Praise the LORD."*

Accept the love He shows.

# Psalm 118

*"It is better to take refuge in the LORD than to trust in man. It is better to take refuge in the LORD than to trust in princes."*

The Lord is my refuge.

# Psalm 119

*"Blessed are they whose ways are blameless, who walk according to the law of the LORD. Blessed are they who keep His statutes and seek Him with all their heart."*

Receive the blessing of the Lord.

# Psalm 120

*"I call on the LORD in my distress,
and He answers me."*

You call - He answers!

# Psalm 121

*"I lift up my eyes to the hills - where does my help come from? My help comes from the LORD, the Maker of heaven and earth."*

Lift up your eyes, help is on the way.

# Psalm 122

*"For the sake of my brothers and friends,
I will say, 'Peace be within you.'"*

Seek peace today.

# Psalm 123

*"Have mercy on us, O LORD, have mercy on us, for we have endured much contempt. We have endured much ridicule from the proud, much contempt from the arrogant."*

May the Lord grant you mercy.

# Psalm 124

*"Our help is in the name of the LORD,
the Maker of heaven and earth."*

Help is yours, receive His help.

# Psalm 125

*"Those who trust in the LORD are like Mount Zion, which cannot be shaken."*

Trust in His unshakable love.

# Psalm 126

*"The LORD has done great things for us, and we are filled with joy."*

Remember the great things the Lord has done for you.

# Psalm 127

*"Unless the LORD builds the house, its builders labor in vain."*

May the Lord build the house of your heart.

# Psalm 128

*"May the LORD bless you from Zion all the days of your life; may you see the prosperity of Jerusalem."*

The Lord grants the blessing of prosperity.

# Psalm 129

*"But the LORD is righteous."*

Seek His righteousness.

# Psalm 130

*"O Israel, put your hope in the LORD for with the LORD is unfailing love and with Him is full redemption."*

As in the days of Israel, place your hope in the Lord.

# Psalm 131

*"But I have stilled and quieted my soul."*

Be still and know that He is God.

# Psalm 132

*"Let us go to His dwelling place; let us worship at His footstool - may Your saints sing for joy."*

Sing for joy!

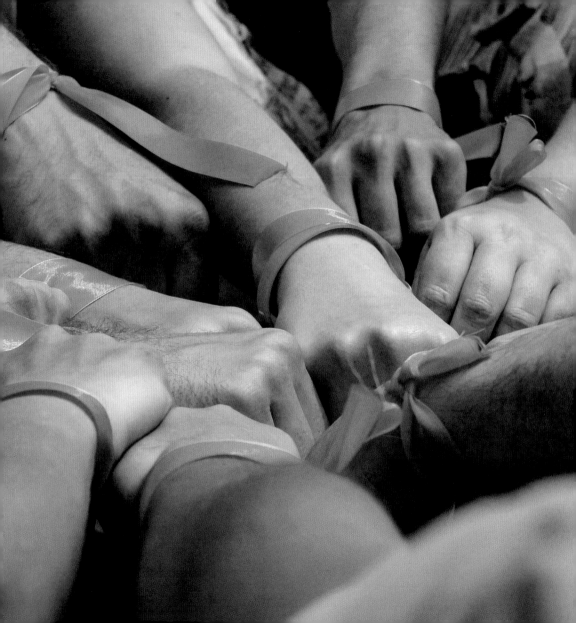

# Psalm 133

*"How good and pleasant it is when brothers live together in unity!"*

Unify in the name of the Lord.

# Psalm 134

*"Lift up your hands in the sanctuary and praise the LORD."*

Lift your hands and your heart to the Lord.

# Psalm 135

*"Praise the LORD, for the LORD is good;*
*sing praise to His name, for that is pleasant."*

May your praise be a pleasant aroma to the Lord.

# Psalm 136

*"Give thanks to the LORD, for He is good. His love endures forever. Give thanks to the God of gods. His love endures forever. Give thanks to the Lord of lords: His love endures forever."*

Thanks be to the Lord our God!

# Psalm 137

*"for there our captors asked us for songs, our
tormentors demanded songs of joy; they said,
'Sing us one of the songs of Zion!"*

In the midst of torment, sing!

# Psalm 138

*"When I called, You answered me; You made me bold and stouthearted."*

Be bold!

# Psalm 139

*"O LORD, You have searched me and You know me... You have laid Your hand upon me."*

He is in control.

# Psalm 140

*"Rescue me, O LORD, from evil men;*
*protect me from men of violence."*

He will protect you and keep you.

# Psalm 141

*"Set a guard over my mouth, O LORD;
keep watch over the door of my lips."*

Let the words of your mouth be pleasing unto the Lord.

# Psalm 142

*"O LORD; I say, 'You are my refuge, my portion in the land of the living.'"*

Take your portion from His plate of plenty.

# Psalm 143

*"Teach me to do Your will, for You are my God; may Your good Spirit lead me on level ground."*

May God make your path straight and level as you walk with Him.

# Psalm 144

*"Blessed are the people of whom this is true;*
*blessed are the people whose God is the LORD."*

Make the Lord your God.

"Great is the LORD and most worthy of praise;
His greatness no one can fathom."

Experience His fathomless greatness.

# Psalm 146

*"The LORD reigns forever, your God, O Zion, for all generations. Praise the LORD."*

Let the Lord reign in your heart.

# Psalm 147

*"Praise the LORD. How good it is to sing praises to our God, how pleasant and fitting to praise Him!"*

Praise Him!

# Psalm 148

*"Praise Him, all His angels, praise Him all His heavenly hosts. Praise Him, sun and moon, praise Him all you shining stars. Praise Him you highest heavens and you waters above the skies."*

Let everything praise the Lord!

# Psalm 149

*"Praise the LORD. Sing to the LORD a new song,
His praise in the assembly of the saints."*

Praise the LORD!

# Psalm 150

*"Praise the LORD. Praise God in His sanctuary; praise Him in His mighty heavens. Praise Him for His acts of power; praise Him for His surpassing greatness. Praise Him with the sounding of the trumpet, praise Him with the harp and lyre, praise Him with tambourine and dancing, praise Him with the strings and flute, praise Him with the clash of cymbals, praise Him with resounding cymbals.*

Let everything that has breath praise the LORD!